M000298306

The Complete REBT Lear

Whether you're learning h[c]

Therapy (REBT) to work i[n]

use it, this program benefits everyone. Comprised of nine booklets, videos, and workbooks, plus an audiocassette album, this program helps every kind of learner through print, sight, and sound.

For the learner . . .

Learn by reading: REBT booklets
- introduce you to the *ABC*'s of REBT
- help you understand your past actions and how you can turn them around

Learn by seeing and hearing: REBT videos and audiocassettes
- see yourself through others—in real-life situations
- review the videos and audios whenever and wherever you want

Learn by doing: REBT workbooks
- test yourself on the workbooks' questions
- practice and develop the skill of using REBT in your everyday life

For the clinician . . .

A cognitive approach: REBT booklets
- begin the phase of defining the problem
- meet your educational needs for both individual and group sessions

An emotive response: REBT videos and audiocassettes
- provide dramatic vignettes and graphic reminders that reinforce core REBT principles
- facilitate group communication, promoting peer-to-peer learning

A behavioral technique: REBT workbooks
- function as effective assessment and evaluation tools
- provide step-by-step guidelines for client goal-setting and goal achievement

For price and order information, or a free catalog, please call our Telephone Representatives.

HAZELDEN
1-800-328-9000 (Toll-Free U.S. and Canada)
1-651-213-4000 (Outside the U.S. and Canada)
1-651-213-4590 (24-Hour Fax)
www.hazelden.org (World Wide Web on the Internet)

15251 Pleasant Valley Road • P.O. Box 176
Center City, MN 55012-0176

The following titles compose the complete REBT learning program. Each is available in booklet, workbook, audio, and video format:

Understanding • *Anger* • *Perfectionism*
Anxiety and Worry • *Depression* • *Shame*
Grief • *Guilt* • *Self-Esteem*

Rational Emotive Behavior Therapy

Shame

Revised

Tim Sheehan, Ph.D.

Hazelden
Center City, Minnesota 55012-0176

ISBN: 1-56838-961-2

The stories in this booklet are composites of many individuals. Any
similarity to any one person is purely coincidental.

About the booklet
This booklet explains where shame comes from and how we use self-
defeating behaviors to dull its pain. It also explains how shame dif-
fers from guilt and how we can cope with it by using the principles
of Rational Emotive Behavior Therapy.

Dr. Albert Ellis, who first articulated Rational-Emotive Therapy
(RET) in the 1950s, changed the name in the 1990s to Rational
Emotive Behavior Therapy (REBT) to more accurately reflect the role
behavior plays in gauging changes in thinking. While the therapeutic
approach remains the same, the pamphlets, workbooks, audios, and
videos in this series have been changed to reflect the updated name.

About the author
Timothy J. Sheehan, Ph.D., is Vice President, Academic Affairs, for
the Hazelden Foundation's Education Division.

Dr. Sheehan holds a Doctorate Degree in Clinical Psychology and
has held numerous positions over the past twenty years at Hazelden,
including leadership roles in clinical psychology and health care ser-
vices, as well as administrative roles in adult, youth, and transitional
care. He is the author of a sequence of pamphlets and workbooks
addressing the application of Rational Emotive Behavior Therapy for
depression and shame as well as *Facing an Eating Disorder in
Recovery* and *Freedom from Compulsion: An Eating Disorder
Workbook*. He is also the author of "The Disease Model" in
McCrady and Epstein's *Addictions: A Comprehensive Guidebook*. He
is a professor in Hazelden's Graduate School in Addiction Studies and
an adjunct associate professor in the graduate school of psychology at
St. Mary's University of Minnesota.

Introduction

Understanding our feelings is no easy task. Most of us have felt the burden of shame at one time or another. Some of us may have been dishonest about our feelings—to ourselves and others—for fear we would be found out or others would know too much. Hurtful feelings frequently surface in recovery, and when we hurt, we feel bad. Words like *miserable* or *sad* can describe these hurtful feelings. Sometimes we not only *feel* bad, we believe we *are* bad. We not only hurt, we also believe something is wrong with the very core of us. We believe something is wrong not only with our use of alcohol or other drugs, but with the core of who we are. We feel something is lacking—we feel inadequate and empty.

That pervasive feeling of chronic emptiness is often *shame*. The void is deepened by self-reproach and a constant longing to be filled. The void of shame is a trap in recovery that robs us of contentment and makes not using alcohol or other drugs or refraining from binge eating and other compulsive behaviors seem impossible.

Where does shame come from?

For most of us, shame has its roots in our childhood. Addiction and emotional problems run in families, and many of us were raised in unhealthy families that did not function well at meeting our emotional, and sometimes our physical, needs. When parents are chronically depressed or overwhelmed in their struggle with an alcohol or other drug dependency, they are often unable to meet the emotional needs of their children. When children do not get their emotional needs met, they often feel shame.

The *ABC* process described in this booklet is based on the work of Dr. Albert Ellis and his Rational Emotive Behavior Therapy.

> Shame is fostered when a child's emotional needs are not met, when that child is not allowed to grow as a valuable person free to explore personal strengths, test individual limits, and embrace himself or herself emotionally.

A nurturing family naturally provides for each member's emotional needs. Children are accepted for who they are; they are cared for and respected. The individuality of family members is maintained. Parents are free to be adults, and children are free to be children.

Shame grows when children and adolescents feel abandoned or neglected, when they are not given adequate care to grow and develop and to value themselves as worthwhile people. These children and adolescents often mature with deeply entrenched beliefs of inadequacy and worthlessness.

Inadequate nurturing during childhood can take a number of different forms. For some of us it was blatant:
- being hit, pushed, or slapped
- being coerced into sexual behavior
- being abandoned for days at a time

For many of us, it was subtle and pervasive:

- being compared with high-achieving brothers and sisters
- being subjected to derogatory remarks about our masculinity or femininity
- being criticized about our ability to achieve or make it on our own
- being criticized about our appearance or weight
- being constantly reminded of mistakes we made
- being threatened that we would turn out just like our "no-good drunken father"

People raised with inadequate nurturing often learn to be vigilant around others lest someone else discovers their feelings of inadequacy. They may feel a need to hide themselves, their emotions, and their thoughts. It becomes important to them to keep secrets, to resist discovery, to avoid making mistakes. Mistakes are seen as the ultimate evidence of worthlessness. A mistake is not viewed as an isolated event, but it is generalized to describe the entire self: *I am a mistake. My shame means that I not only* feel *bad, but that I believe I am bad, inadequate, and flawed.*

This sort of reasoning promotes a vicious cycle where children who aren't *valued* often mature to adulthood believing they are not *valuable.* To hide their feelings of worthlessness, they develop a rigid defense system. No one is to find out about them. Hints of inadequacy are cautiously guarded. They deny and distrust their emotions and no longer freely express their feelings, show affection, or feel comfortable with their sexuality. Chronic unhappiness, apathy, and anticipation of being found out take the place of feelings of trust and sharing.

Shame and chemical dependency

Shame can also be learned later in life. Those of us who struggle with a drug addiction can despair over our emotional problems as the addictive cycle escalates and eventually defeats our attempts to lead a healthier, more productive life. Robbed of our feelings of hope, this self-defeating cycle only underscores our behavior problems and exaggerates our feelings of worthlessness.

Self-defeating behavior

Ellen has been drug- and alcohol-free for the last six months, yet she is overwhelmed by chronic feelings of emptiness and self-doubt. She feels paralyzed and can't

identify or express her feelings. She fears that her lack of worth will be transparent. She no longer has her pills and alcohol to fill the void. For self-protection, Ellen relies on a rigid defense mechanism, and vows to herself that no one will learn of her feelings of utter worthlessness and shame; no one will know her secret. Instead, Ellen strives to be "perfect."

Ellen's reliance on perfectionism is a frequently used defense against shame. Perfectionism is actually a rigid belief system, "a judge within," that monitors, evaluates, and critiques our behavior, thoughts, and feelings. The judge within demands perfection. Mistakes are disastrous! We think we must achieve in all areas of our lives to be worthwhile. We convince ourselves that only a perfect performance will compensate for our inward feelings of shame.

Ellen is caught between two unrealistic demands: her never-ending and impossible striving for perfect behavior, and her insistence that she keep her shameful feelings secret. She is in a no-win situation. Although Ellen has stopped using pills, her shame continues to motivate perfectionistic behaviors that limit her ability to seek the help she so desperately needs.

Jim is haunted by a nagging feeling of inadequacy. Outwardly, he projects an image of self-confidence. Inwardly, however, he feels incomplete. He secretly takes one drink after another in a futile effort to quell his addiction, to fill his persistent feelings of emptiness and quiet his feelings of shame. The more he tries to numb his feelings, the emptier he feels.

> Self-defeating behavior dulls our pain or helps us to feel good momentarily, but it doesn't solve any of our problems.

Jim's addiction seems—at least temporarily—to fill the void of shame. But like Ellen, who relies on perfectionism to mask her shame, Jim eventually deepens his feelings of worthlessness by drinking. Both Jim's and Ellen's responses to shame are self-defeating. Jim's dependence on alcohol dulls his perception of shame but only for a time. Ellen avoids her feelings of shame but defeats her purpose of getting help for her emotional turmoil by maintaining a rigid facade of perfectionism.

Shame and its self-defeating consequences

Shame is an emotional problem. Emotions are problems when they block us from reaching some of our most basic goals. For many of us, building a more healthy lifestyle involves developing fulfilling relationships by allowing ourselves to be vulnerable and imperfect with those we trust and accepting the vulnerability and imperfections of others. To be human is to be fallible and less than perfect. Recovery also means actively participating in the world of work, taking joy in living day to day and, of course, remaining abstinent. When a feeling such as shame blocks us from fulfilling one of these basic tasks, we have an emotional problem.

Shame is therefore an obstacle to learning the basic tasks of living. Feelings of chronic emptiness can undermine our efforts to feel content and can give us an excuse for relapse. Shame keeps us isolated and separated from others, thus sabotaging our needs for intimacy and meaningful relationships. It interferes with our capacity to relate to others as whole, imperfect persons.

Shame is a special problem for people recovering from addictions and emotional problems. If we have unidentified feelings of shame that are not dealt with, we are at risk for relapse. In fact, how we behave when we feel ashamed is often the opposite of how we behave in recovery. Recovery is the process by which we are restored to a more fulfilling life that often involves fewer emotional hardships and freedom from addictive behavior.

Characteristics of shame	Recovery characteristics
Seeks social isolation and emotional withdrawal.	Participates in the social process of recovery.
Feels lack of trust in oneself.	Trusts one's opinions and feelings.
Experiences constricted spontaneity.	Experiences joy.
Repeats similar mistakes.	Learns from past experience.
Relies on rigid behaviors.	Approaches problems with flexibility.

Since shame feels bad and results in our self-defeating behaviors, it is important that we identify and reduce our shame as part of our process of recovery.

Shame versus guilt
Shame is different from guilt. Guilt is a reactive feeling to a misbehavior, or an omission of an expected behavior. For example, an adolescent may feel guilty because he or she acted in ways that hurt others, or a father may feel guilty because he has neglected his son. Guilt is usually limited to a specific event and doesn't involve an evaluation of our basic worth as people. In fact, feelings of guilt are often healthy. They can be a signal to us that we've missed something or need to take a closer look at our behavior. We can learn to appreciate guilt, not fear it. It reminds us that we are imperfect, worthwhile humans able to learn from our mistakes and grow as fully functioning people.

In contrast, feelings of shame usually involve our sense of worth as people.

> Shame is not a simple reaction to a specific event; rather, it is a learned emotional response that lingers no matter how good our performance might be.

When we feel shameful we are likely to isolate ourselves and to withdraw emotionally; we are less likely to be spontaneous and to feel joy. The self-defeating behaviors of shame reinforce unrelenting feelings of distress, emptiness, and worthlessness.

The good news
Feelings of shame can be changed! Since shame is learned, it can be unlearned and replaced by more positive attitudes, behaviors, and feelings. We can lessen our feelings of shame by understanding their roots, by acknowledging that we feel shame, and by consciously changing shame-related behaviors.

> Beliefs about our self, learned either early in childhood or later in life, tend to persist even when our addiction has stopped.

As children, we tend to believe what adults teach us, particularly when these adults are considered trustworthy—such as parents, clergy, or teachers. As adolescents, we modify our attitudes based on our experiences. Thus, if we are faced with continued failures, criticism, and our own early addictive behaviors, we soon learn to devalue our worth. Children and adolescents, by the nature of their youth, lack the necessary skills, knowledge, and emotional stability to understand the complexity of their attitudes and feelings. Consequently, we aren't responsible for how we were treated in the past or how we learned early on to feel about ourselves. In essence, we are not responsible for our childhood. By nature, childhood is characterized by powerlessness.

The same is true for addiction and compulsive behaviors. Some of us have experienced obsessions and compulsive behaviors that have invaded every part of our personality; others of us have experienced a loss of control over certain behaviors such as drinking or gambling. All of us have faced and felt the continued defeat and destruction from our inability to change our behavior. Firm resolve and willpower alone have often resulted in dismal failure. Although we wanted the pain of our self-defeating behavior to stop, we were powerless. Like children, we were powerless in our attempts to control the complexities of our attitudes, feelings, and addictive behavior.

It is only by accepting our powerlessness as adults that we are empowered to recover. As recovering people, we are more aware of our feelings and can make conscious choices about what we think and how we behave. Shame is perpetuated by our belief systems. No matter when, where, or how we learned them, these shame-based attitudes are now our own. The judge within who represents our perfectionistic strivings to control can be disputed, diminished, and eventually kicked off the bench! The judge's rule is not absolute and can be diffused with persistent opposition based on logic and reason.

REBT principles

While our shame may be rooted in the past, we need to cope with it in the present. One method to attack shame-based attitudes is to utilize a self-help approach: Rational Emotive Behavior Therapy (REBT). The premise of REBT is that thoughts trigger feelings. Many of us think of our feelings as an automatic reaction to isolated events. We often talk about our uncomfortable feelings as if someone or something else were responsible for them: "She made me angry." Many of us believe that events at *A* cause emotions at *B*.

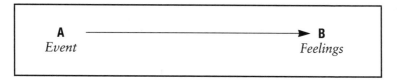

Feelings aren't automatic, however, nor are feelings necessarily similar or consistent in response to similar events. For instance, an event (*A*), such as receiving feedback in group, might result in a number of different feelings (*B*), ranging from sadness to anger. So feelings vary from individual to individual and are not automatically linked to events. Thus, emotions are not directly caused by events. REBT says that we can choose how to interpret or think about the event at *B* which in turn causes a feeling at *C*.

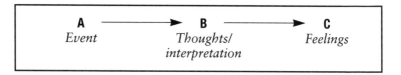

Ellen's story

Although sober for six months, Ellen has been crippled by continual nightmares, sleepless nights, and relationship problems. She has sought the support of a women's therapy group. While she has mustered the courage to ask for help, she feels numb and unable to share her feelings. Ellen has relied for so long on a perfectionistic defense, keeping others at a safe distance, that it is now difficult to let others in.

Now journaling the events of her childhood, Ellen recalls a long-suppressed family history involving painful feelings and physical abuse. Both of Ellen's parents had been alcoholics. Ellen is filled with a surge of shame and subsequently dreads telling her story. As she thinks of her past, Ellen tells herself, *I should have been able to stop the abuse. I shouldn't have put up with it for so long. What an unlovable child I must have been to deserve such abuse. What an awful adult I've become. No one must know.*

A → *Event*	B → *Thoughts*	C *Feelings*	*Behavioral consequences*
Telling the story.	I should have stopped the abuse. I shouldn't have put up with it. What an unlovable child I must have been. What an awful adult I've become. No one must ever know.	shame	Isolated from peers, avoids telling her story.

As a result of her shame, Ellen attempts to isolate herself in group. Her behavior is self-defeating, since she eliminates the emotional support that she needs to face her secret. Ellen's belief system (B) is characterized by unrealistic demands further compounded by a tendency to "awfulize" herself. Ellen's "should's" and "must's" signify her unrealistic demands that she should have had more power or

B ⟶	C ⟶	D
Thoughts	*Feelings*	*Critique*
I should have stopped the abuse.	shame	*Who* says I should have stopped the abuse? I was a child. I had no more power over my parents than they had over their drinking.
I shouldn't have put up with it.	shame	*What* choices did I have? Aren't we all powerless as children? I'm not responsible for my parents' behavior. Stop making unrealistic demands!
What an unlovable child I must have been.	shame	*What* evidence do I have that I was an unlovable child? Aren't all children lovable and worthy? Aren't all children deserving of love and care?
What an awful adult I've become.	shame	Just because I was criticized in the past is no reason to criticize myself now. Sure, I'm not perfect, but who is? Aren't we all worthwhile, fallible humans?
No one must ever know.	shame	*Why?* I'm not responsible for my childhood. Aren't my parents responsible for their behavior? Because I was abused in the past is no proof that I am a worthless adult now.

control. In turn, she debases her own worth by blaming herself and undermining her value as a person. Ellen interprets her past events through a filter of shame-inducing beliefs. The judge within formulates rigid expectations for Ellen's performance and shames her when she is unable to reach these unattainable goals.

Fortunately for Ellen, two of her peers helped to draw her out by sharing their stories in group. Eventually, Ellen learned to dispute her shame-based logic (D) by raising such questions as *who? what?* and *why?*

Setting goals
As Ellen's logic begins to change, she is free to identify her goals. While her emptiness and shame will not disappear overnight, she is more comfortable and less upset more of the time. She has formulated a goal of living a productive, healthy life with as little shame as possible. To help reach her goals, Ellen is continuing to participate in her women's therapy group and is beginning individual therapy. In the meantime, Ellen is renewing her emerging attitude of self-respect with an affirmation:

I am Ellen, a fallible, worthwhile person deserving of self-respect and the respect of others. Today I will treat myself as a worthy, deserving person.

Since Ellen's judge within is not easily disputed, she has designed a concrete plan to help her use her new affirmation. As a reminder, she pairs her self-affirmation to a frequent daily activity. Since she drinks four sodas each day, Ellen has decided to use her first sip as a cue to repeat her positive affirmation. Once she completes her self-affirmation, Ellen drinks the remainder of the soda as a reward for her new attitude.

Later, Ellen draws up a list of shame-attacking activities with the help of her group therapist. While Ellen understands some of her shame-based attitudes, she also understood that her chronic feelings of emptiness could easily put her at risk for relapse into her old self-defeating behavior. Though she is feeling comfortable more of the time, she knows that her issues involving shame are not completely resolved.

Ellen has also decided to continue educating herself about shame. She has planned a special reading assignment,

and she has found a therapist who is versed in both addiction and childhood abuse issues. Ellen plans to continue with her daily schedule of self-affirmations. Since she is also planning to attend her women's therapy group, Ellen has decided to complete at least two additional REBT assignments so she will be better able to discuss her shame-based attitudes with her peers.

Ellen's shame is obviously rooted in childhood experiences, and her "awfulizing" attitudes about these experiences and about herself could have obstructed her progress. But by disputing her shaming logic, Ellen has empowered herself to make the changes she needs.

Jim's story

In contrast, Jim's shame does not result from childhood experiences, but is instead directly related to the self-defeating consequences of addiction. The more he drinks, the less he values himself. Although he strives to control his drinking, his efforts are a dismal failure time after time.

According to Jim, he should be able to control his drinking. Jim fervently believes that he is bad or worthless because he can't stop or reduce his drinking.

Jim can predict neither intervals of abstinence nor intoxication. He begins to see himself as a moral degenerate. Jim thinks if he had value or worth he would not degrade himself through continued intoxication and public humiliation. As Jim's shame mounts, he withdraws even further from his friends and family. He then drinks more in his isolation.

Jim's belief that he is worthless is based on his demand that he *should* be able to control his drinking. The judge within demands willpower and self-restraint and condemns Jim's worth when he is unable to control his behavior. Jim's shame and isolation are obstacles to his recovery—he shuts out all those who could be of help.

A ──▶	B ──▶	C	Behavioral
Event	*Thoughts*	*Feelings*	*consequences*
Contin-ued drinking	I absolutely *should* be able to control my drinking.	shame	Social isolation, continued drinking.
	It's *awful* that I can't handle even one drink.		
	I'm simply a *bad* person.		

Jim's family and friends didn't give up. Through their support and understanding, Jim eventually agreed to treatment. However, the judge within continued to demand perfect control. Jim held onto his unrealistic demand that he should be able to control his drinking. Through concerted efforts from peers, and education regarding alcoholism, Jim began to dispute his logic at (D).

B ──▶	C ──▶	D
Thoughts	*Feelings*	*Critique*
I absolutely *should* be able to control my drinking.	shame	*Who* says I should be able to control my drinking? Isn't alcoholism a disease? Disease is not a matter of willpower.
It's *awful* that I can't handle even one drink.	shame	Of course I can't handle just one drink. My drinking isn't a matter of voluntary control. Once I take one drink, I'm bound to finish the bottle.
I'm simply a *bad* person.	shame	Stop "awfulizing"! I have a bad disease. I am not a bad person.

As Jim's beliefs about his alcoholism began to change, he became increasingly aware of his unrealistic demands of himself. In accepting his powerlessness over alcohol, Jim also accepted his own humanity with all its strengths and limitations. Jim's shame is rooted in his belief that he needs to control the uncontrollable. For Jim to recognize his limitations as a human is an ongoing task—he is no longer striving to be perfect.

Taking action
As Jim progressed, his counselor made a number of helpful recommendations. In order to reduce his shame, Jim needed to become more flexible in his expectations of himself and others. Since Jim had accepted himself as a fallible, worthwhile human, there was no longer any reason for him to listen to his judge within. His lack of control and powerlessness were no longer threats to his worth, but simply characteristics of being human. Any efforts to control the uncontrollable could only lead to failure and often to self-reproach and shame. With this in mind, Jim agreed to incorporate the following activities.

Finding a support group. Jim identified a need for ongoing support from a group that could help point out some of his shame-based thinking and self-defeating behavior. He understood that his attitudes often involved a need to control that easily sabotaged his acceptance of his alcoholism. Jim agreed to explore at least two different groups—AA and a men's support group.

Completing an REBT assignment. Prior to his discharge from treatment, Jim also completed an additional REBT assignment to dispute his demandingness, or what his counselor referred to as "shoulding." Jim learned that words such as *must* or *should* often represent unrealistic demands and are key words to dispute when changing attitudes. With this in mind, Jim began to work on his REBT assignment on feelings of shame that related to his marriage.

Jim wrote down "shame" as an emotional problem under C (Feelings). Jim knew that his feelings of shame were closely linked to both social isolation and drinking. Under A (Event), Jim identified a recent event that sparked his awareness of his shameful feelings—he remembered that his last visit with his wife was an occasion of intense shame. Jim reflected on his thoughts in response to his wife's visit, and wrote them out under B (Thoughts):

- I should be able to fix my wife's feelings.
- It's awful to see her cry.
- I should have known better than to become an alcoholic.
- What a miserable person I am.

Understanding the basic tools of REBT, Jim disputed his logic by writing a critique of his thinking under D (Dispute).

- Who says I should be able to fix my wife's feelings? I can't control her emotions.
- It's unpleasant to see her cry, and I wish she didn't have to go through this. Perhaps her tears will bring her some emotional relief.
- Alcoholism is rooted in my biological makeup. It's not a matter of willpower. Stop "shoulding" on yourself!
- I'm a fallible, worthwhile human. I have been struggling with this miserable disease. I'm not a miserable person.

As Jim questioned his own thinking, he formulated a goal to help guide his behavior (E). Jim recognized his need to provide emotional support to his wife while reducing his shame. Consequently, he listed the following constructive actions he could take to reach his goal:

- Express my concern and support directly to my wife.
- Invite her to participate in a couples' communications workshop at the local mental health center.
- Support my wife's involvement in a support group that addresses her needs.
- Complete two additional REBT worksheets to identify specific ways I continue to shame myself.

Jim soon learned that by consciously challenging his beliefs and changing his behaviors, he was able to reduce his feelings of shame while providing emotional support to his wife. As Jim accepted his powerlessness over alcohol, he also recognized his other limitations. He was indeed fallible, but certainly not "bad" or "awful." Jim came to believe that it was human to make mistakes, to have limited control over one's life, and to have an illness like alcoholism. By accepting his humanity, Jim took an important first step in building a foundation for recovery while alleviating his self-reproach, unrealistic demands, and feelings of shame.

Putting it all together

Here are six important things to remember about shame:

1. Shame is a pervasive feeling of worthlessness. Shame is different from guilt; it is not a simple reaction to our misbehavior. Shame is often a chronic feeling of inadequacy, emptiness, and self-doubt.

2. Shame is often rooted in childhood and adolescence, stemming from an unhealthy family system. The child or adolescent believes that severe family criticism is justified and grows up believing he or she is without worth or value. We were powerless over what we learned as a child.

3. Shame can also be a consequence of addiction. The inability to stop or control an addictive behavior frequently leads us to devalue our worth.

4. Intense feelings of shame result in self-defeating behaviors such as social withdrawal or isolation, and addictive behavior such as binge eating, compulsive gambling, or excessive drinking. Therefore, shame is a risk factor for relapse.

5. Shame usually involves a judge within who demands rigid performance and shames us when these demands go unmet. Shame often involves a swing from perfectionistic expectations to self-condemnation. The "judge within" actually represents our own belief systems.

6. Since shame is invented and learned, it can be un-invented and unlearned. By using resources available to us including basic REBT tools, we can successfully reduce our feelings of shame—that is, experience shame less intensely and less often.

An REBT assignment

Now it's your turn! As with any new behavior, you need to practice reducing your feelings of shame. Your task is to complete an REBT assignment. You may want to use a notebook. Here are a few tips to consider as you write out an assignment.

Identify shame. First, start by identifying the upsetting feeling of shame. Consider the self-defeating behaviors commonly related to shame. Be specific. Think of an example from your own experience.

Identify the event. Next, identify the activating event. Think of a time when a particular action encouraged you to feel shame more intensely. It might have been feedback during group therapy, or a comment that your spouse made. In any event, be as objective, concrete, and specific as possible in identifying the event (A).

Identify your thoughts and feelings. Your next task is to identify your thoughts (B). Review the examples of Ellen and Jim. Usually, feelings of shame (C) are triggered by unrealistic demands, a tendency to "awfulize," and self-devaluation.

Critique your thinking. Dispute your logic (D). Here, critique your thoughts, question your logic, and develop a more rational alternative.

State your goals. Consider your goals for the situation. Of course, you prefer to feel shame less often and less intensely. It's better to allow yourself to feel sorry and regretful instead of shamed and self-doubting. Reducing shame is certainly an important goal for a contented recovery. Often, this goal helps to guide us in acting constructively.

Taking action. List all the constructive actions you could take in order to reach your goal (E). Be as specific and concrete as possible. Number that list and keep it simple, but focus on action.

Now that you have completed a written REBT assignment, your next task is to share this assignment with others. Look for additional feedback regarding your thinking (B). Ask your peers if there is something you've missed. Might they have additional ideas for disputing your logic (D)? Perhaps one of your peers has an additional action to list under E. Use the REBT assignment as a catalyst in discussing your feelings, shame-based attitudes, and emerging alternative belief systems. The more you involve others in the process, the more quickly you are likely to learn ways to reduce feelings of shame.

Don't forget to consider other self-help methods in attacking your feelings of shame. Remember, Ellen used self-affirmations to reinforce her emerging attitude of self-respect. Jim, for instance, identified ways that he "took control" and blocked acceptance of both his alcoholism and his humanity. Both Jim and Ellen took care to inform their sponsors that shame was a relapse risk.

Don't give up easily. You've probably had many years of practicing shame-based behaviors. It will take a lot of practice to find new self-affirming behaviors. A number of resources can be helpful, such as self-help support groups, individual and group therapy, long-term counseling, and relapse-prevention groups. By modifying attitudes and changing behavior, you can reduce your feelings of shame, lessen your risk for relapse, and open yourself to the joys of a healthier, happier life.